This Journal Belongs to

If found, please phone

Table of content	
Gardening Projects	3
Plant wish list	4-5
Garden layouts	6-9
Plant profiles	10-32
Season checklists, Monthly and weekly Planner	33-144
Gardening expenses	112-115
Planting tracker	116-121
Garden year in review	122

All the steps in this notebook are simple guides, not rules. We highly recommend that you find different sources to study the topic.

Although, the publisher and author have used their best efforts in Writing and preparing this journal, guide and planner, they make no representations or warranties with respect to the accuracy or completeness of the contents of this document. The information is to be used at your own risk. The author cannot guarantee any specific outcomes that may result from using the methods outlined in the following pages.

Gardening Projects

My dream garden looks and feels like

New projects for this year are

Techniques I may use

Notes

Plant Wish list

Which plants would you like to grow?

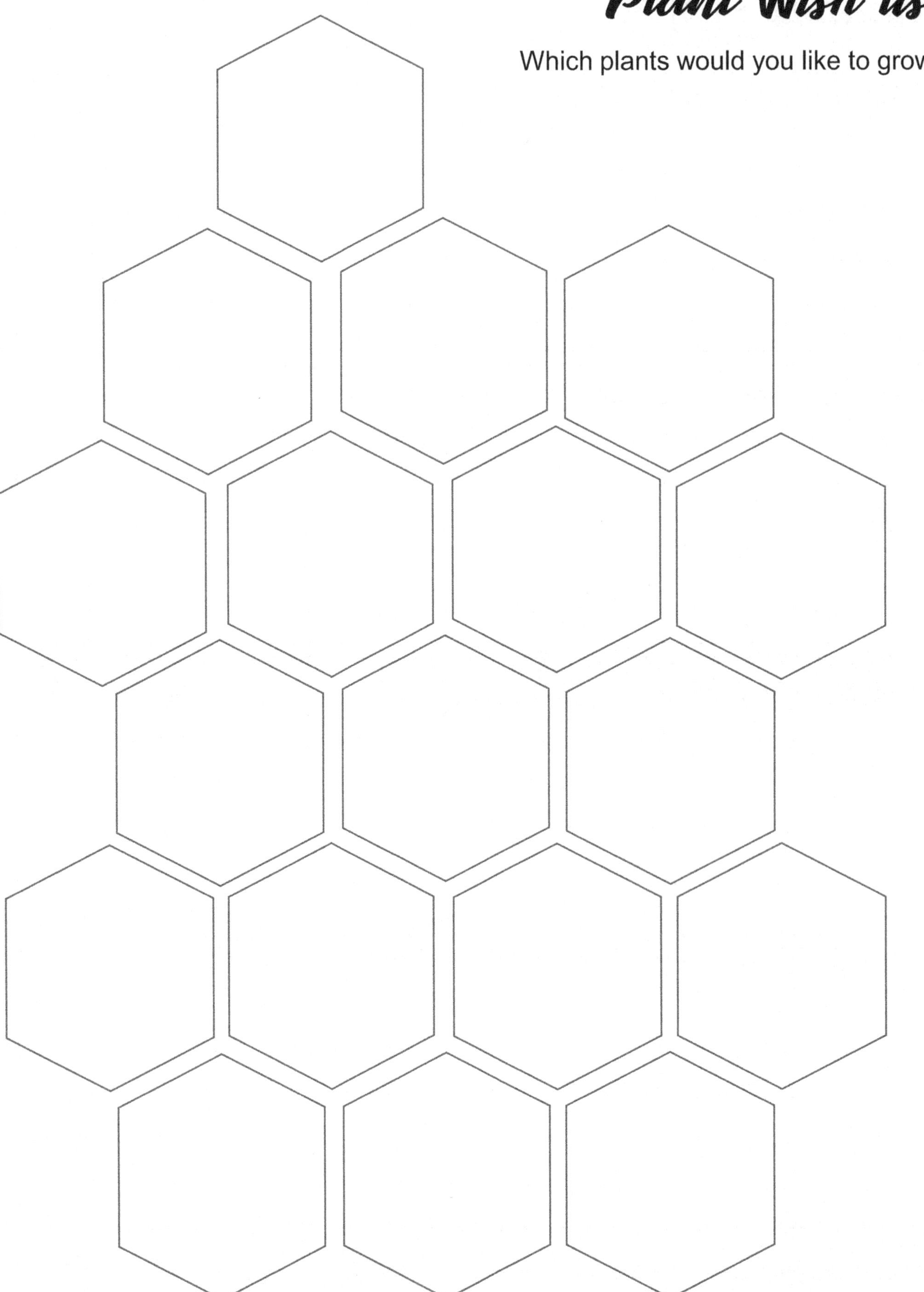

Plant Wish list

Garden Layout

Garden Layout

Garden Layout

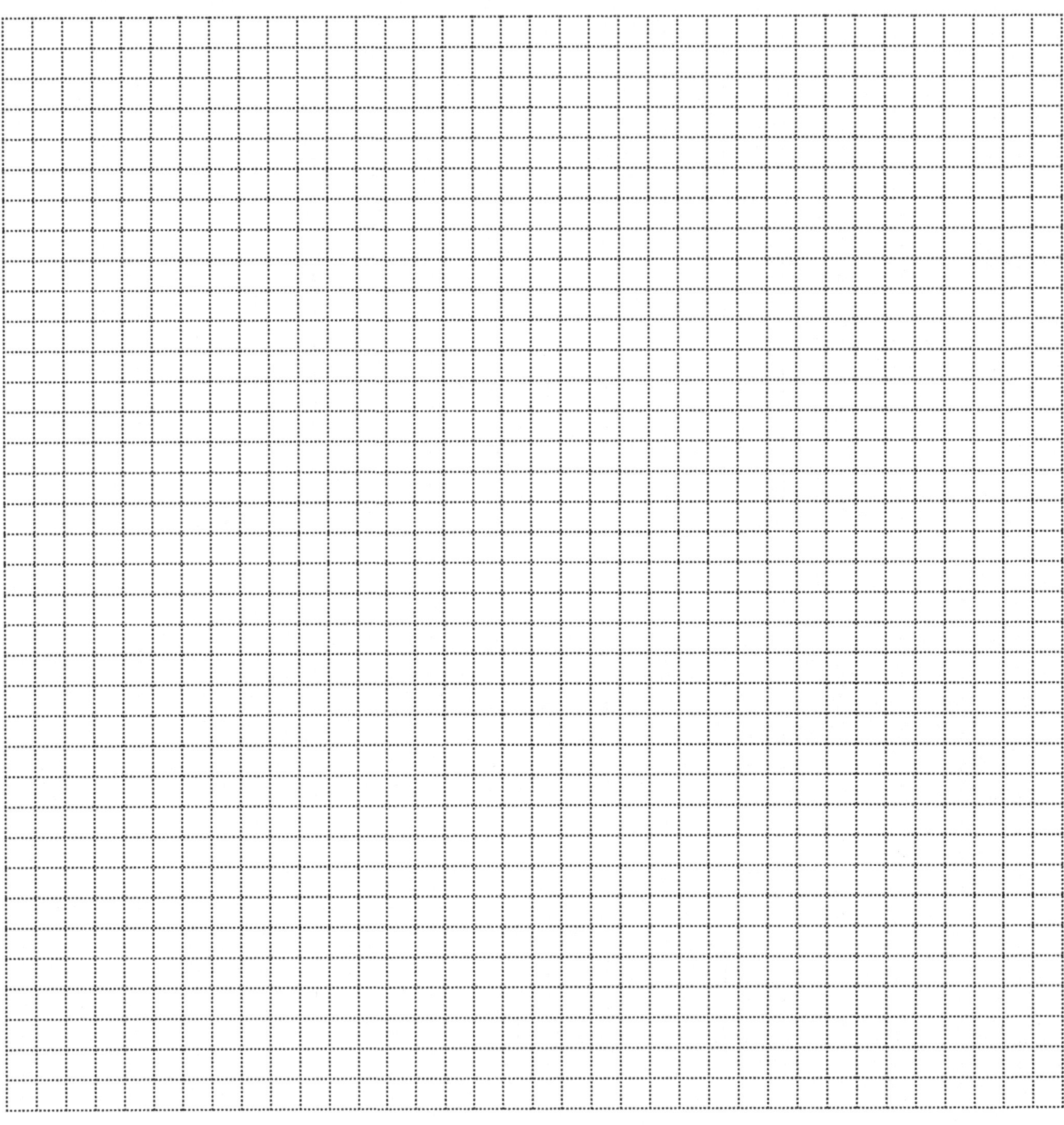

Garden Layout

Plant Profiles

Plant		Page	Plant		Page

Name	
Purchased at	Price
Type (fruit, Vegetable, herb, etc)	
Date germinated	Date planted
Location planted	Harvest date
Planting instructions	
Care instructions	
Harvest instructions	
Pests/ problems	
Notes	

Name	
Purchased at	Price
Type (fruit, Vegetable, herb, etc)	
Date germinated	Date planted
Location planted	Harvest date
Planting instructions	
Care instructions	
Harvest instructions	
Pests/ problems	
Notes	

Name	
Purchased at	Price
Type (fruit, Vegetable, herb, etc)	
Date germinated	Date planted
Location planted	Harvest date
Planting instructions	
Care instructions	
Harvest instructions	
Pests/ problems	
Notes	

Name	
Purchased at	Price
Type (fruit, Vegetable, herb, etc)	
Date germinated	Date planted
Location planted	Harvest date
Planting instructions	
Care instructions	
Harvest instructions	
Pests/ problems	
Notes	

Name	
Purchased at	Price
Type (fruit, Vegetable, herb, etc)	
Date germinated	Date planted
Location planted	Harvest date
Planting instructions	
Care instructions	
Harvest instructions	
Pests/ problems	
Notes	

Name	
Purchased at	Price
Type (fruit, Vegetable, herb, etc)	
Date germinated	Date planted
Location planted	Harvest date
Planting instructions	
Care instructions	
Harvest instructions	
Pests/ problems	
Notes	

Name	
Purchased at	Price
Type (fruit, Vegetable, herb, etc)	
Date germinated	Date planted
Location planted	Harvest date
Planting instructions	
Care instructions	
Harvest instructions	
Pests/ problems	
Notes	

Name	
Purchased at	Price
Type (fruit, Vegetable, herb, etc)	
Date germinated	Date planted
Location planted	Harvest date
Planting instructions	
Care instructions	
Harvest instructions	
Pests/ problems	
Notes	

Name	
Purchased at	Price
Type (fruit, Vegetable, herb, etc)	
Date germinated	Date planted
Location planted	Harvest date
Planting instructions	
Care instructions	
Harvest instructions	
Pests/ problems	
Notes	

Name	
Purchased at	Price
Type (fruit, Vegetable, herb, etc)	
Date germinated	Date planted
Location planted	Harvest date
Planting instructions	
Care instructions	
Harvest instructions	
Pests/ problems	
Notes	

Name	
Purchased at	Price
Type (fruit, Vegetable, herb, etc)	
Date germinated	Date planted
Location planted	Harvest date
Planting instructions	
Care instructions	
Harvest instructions	
Pests/ problems	
Notes	

Name	
Purchased at	Price
Type (fruit, Vegetable, herb, etc)	
Date germinated	Date planted
Location planted	Harvest date
Planting instructions	
Care instructions	
Harvest instructions	
Pests/ problems	
Notes	

Name	
Purchased at	Price
Type (fruit, Vegetable, herb, etc)	
Date germinated	Date planted
Location planted	Harvest date
Planting instructions	
Care instructions	
Harvest instructions	
Pests/ problems	
Notes	

Name	
Purchased at	Price
Type (fruit, Vegetable, herb, etc)	
Date germinated	Date planted
Location planted	Harvest date
Planting instructions	
Care instructions	
Harvest instructions	
Pests/ problems	
Notes	

Name	
Purchased at	Price
Type (fruit, Vegetable, herb, etc)	
Date germinated	Date planted
Location planted	Harvest date
Planting instructions	
Care instructions	
Harvest instructions	
Pests/ problems	
Notes	

Name	
Purchased at	Price
Type (fruit, Vegetable, herb, etc)	
Date germinated	Date planted
Location planted	Harvest date
Planting instructions	
Care instructions	
Harvest instructions	
Pests/ problems	
Notes	

Name	
Purchased at	Price
Type (fruit, Vegetable, herb, etc)	
Date germinated	Date planted
Location planted	Harvest date
Planting instructions	
Care instructions	
Harvest instructions	
Pests/ problems	
Notes	

Name	
Purchased at	Price
Type (fruit, Vegetable, herb, etc)	
Date germinated	Date planted
Location planted	Harvest date
Planting instructions	
Care instructions	
Harvest instructions	
Pests/ problems	
Notes	

Name	
Purchased at	Price
Type (fruit, Vegetable, herb, etc)	
Date germinated	Date planted
Location planted	Harvest date
Planting instructions	
Care instructions	
Harvest instructions	
Pests/ problems	
Notes	

Name	
Purchased at	Price
Type (fruit, Vegetable, herb, etc)	
Date germinated	Date planted
Location planted	Harvest date
Planting instructions	
Care instructions	
Harvest instructions	
Pests/ problems	
Notes	

Name	
Purchased at	Price
Type (fruit, Vegetable, herb, etc)	
Date germinated	Date planted
Location planted	Harvest date
Planting instructions	
Care instructions	
Harvest instructions	
Pests/ problems	
Notes	

Name	
Purchased at	Price
Type (fruit, Vegetable, herb, etc)	
Date germinated	Date planted
Location planted	Harvest date
Planting instructions	
Care instructions	
Harvest instructions	
Pests/ problems	
Notes	

Name	
Purchased at	Price
Type (fruit, Vegetable, herb, etc)	
Date germinated	Date planted
Location planted	Harvest date
Planting instructions	
Care instructions	
Harvest instructions	
Pests/ problems	
Notes	

Name	
Purchased at	Price
Type (fruit, Vegetable, herb, etc)	
Date germinated	Date planted
Location planted	Harvest date
Planting instructions	
Care instructions	
Harvest instructions	
Pests/ problems	
Notes	

Name	
Purchased at	Price
Type (fruit, Vegetable, herb, etc)	
Date germinated	Date planted
Location planted	Harvest date
Planting instructions	
Care instructions	
Harvest instructions	
Pests/ problems	
Notes	

Name	
Purchased at	Price
Type (fruit, Vegetable, herb, etc)	
Date germinated	Date planted
Location planted	Harvest date
Planting instructions	
Care instructions	
Harvest instructions	
Pests/ problems	
Notes	

Name	
Purchased at	Price
Type (fruit, Vegetable, herb, etc)	
Date germinated	Date planted
Location planted	Harvest date
Planting instructions	
Care instructions	
Harvest instructions	
Pests/ problems	
Notes	

Name	
Purchased at	Price
Type (fruit, Vegetable, herb, etc)	
Date germinated	Date planted
Location planted	Harvest date
Planting instructions	
Care instructions	
Harvest instructions	
Pests/ problems	
Notes	

Name	
Purchased at	Price
Type (fruit, Vegetable, herb, etc)	
Date germinated	Date planted
Location planted	Harvest date
Planting instructions	
Care instructions	
Harvest instructions	
Pests/ problems	
Notes	

Name	
Purchased at	Price
Type (fruit, Vegetable, herb, etc)	
Date germinated	Date planted
Location planted	Harvest date
Planting instructions	
Care instructions	
Harvest instructions	
Pests/ problems	
Notes	

Name	
Purchased at	Price
Type (fruit, Vegetable, herb, etc)	
Date germinated	Date planted
Location planted	Harvest date
Planting instructions	
Care instructions	
Harvest instructions	
Pests/ problems	
Notes	

Name	
Purchased at	Price
Type (fruit, Vegetable, herb, etc)	
Date germinated	Date planted
Location planted	Harvest date
Planting instructions	
Care instructions	
Harvest instructions	
Pests/ problems	
Notes	

Name	
Purchased at	Price
Type (fruit, Vegetable, herb, etc)	
Date germinated	Date planted
Location planted	Harvest date
Planting instructions	
Care instructions	
Harvest instructions	
Pests/ problems	
Notes	

Name	
Purchased at	Price
Type (fruit, Vegetable, herb, etc)	
Date germinated	Date planted
Location planted	Harvest date
Planting instructions	
Care instructions	
Harvest instructions	
Pests/ problems	
Notes	

Name	
Purchased at	Price
Type (fruit, Vegetable, herb, etc)	
Date germinated	Date planted
Location planted	Harvest date
Planting instructions	
Care instructions	
Harvest instructions	
Pests/ problems	
Notes	

Name	
Purchased at	Price
Type (fruit, Vegetable, herb, etc)	
Date germinated	Date planted
Location planted	Harvest date
Planting instructions	
Care instructions	
Harvest instructions	
Pests/ problems	
Notes	

Name	
Purchased at	Price
Type (fruit, Vegetable, herb, etc)	
Date germinated	Date planted
Location planted	Harvest date
Planting instructions	
Care instructions	
Harvest instructions	
Pests/ problems	
Notes	

Name	
Purchased at	Price
Type (fruit, Vegetable, herb, etc)	
Date germinated	Date planted
Location planted	Harvest date
Planting instructions	
Care instructions	
Harvest instructions	
Pests/ problems	
Notes	

Name	
Purchased at	Price
Type (fruit, Vegetable, herb, etc)	
Date germinated	Date planted
Location planted	Harvest date
Planting instructions	
Care instructions	
Harvest instructions	
Pests/ problems	
Notes	

Name	
Purchased at	Price
Type (fruit, Vegetable, herb, etc)	
Date germinated	Date planted
Location planted	Harvest date
Planting instructions	
Care instructions	
Harvest instructions	
Pests/ problems	
Notes	

Name	
Purchased at	Price
Type (fruit, Vegetable, herb, etc)	
Date germinated	Date planted
Location planted	Harvest date
Planting instructions	
Care instructions	
Harvest instructions	
Pests/ problems	
Notes	

Name	
Purchased at	Price
Type (fruit, Vegetable, herb, etc)	
Date germinated	Date planted
Location planted	Harvest date
Planting instructions	
Care instructions	
Harvest instructions	
Pests/ problems	
Notes	

Name	
Purchased at	Price
Type (fruit, Vegetable, herb, etc)	
Date germinated	Date planted
Location planted	Harvest date
Planting instructions	
Care instructions	
Harvest instructions	
Pests/ problems	
Notes	

Name	
Purchased at	Price
Type (fruit, Vegetable, herb, etc)	
Date germinated	Date planted
Location planted	Harvest date
Planting instructions	
Care instructions	
Harvest instructions	
Pests/ problems	
Notes	

Season Checklist

Monthly Planner

Weekly Chores

Weekly Chores

Weekly Chores

Weekly Chores

Monthly Planner

Weekly Chores

Weekly Chores

Weekly Chores

Weekly Chores	

Monthly Planner

Weekly Chores

Weekly Chores

Weekly Chores

Weekly Chores

Notes

Season Checklist

Monthly Planner

Weekly Chores

Weekly Chores

Weekly Chores

Weekly Chores

Monthly Planner

Weekly Chores

Weekly Chores

Weekly Chores

Weekly Chores

Monthly Planner

Weekly Chores

Weekly Chores

Weekly Chores

Weekly Chores

Notes

Season Checklist

Monthly Planner

Weekly Chores

Weekly Chores

Weekly Chores

Weekly Chores

Monthly Planner

Weekly Chores

Weekly Chores

Weekly Chores

Weekly Chores

Monthly Planner

Weekly Chores

Weekly Chores

Weekly Chores

Weekly Chores

Monthly Planner

Weekly Chores

Weekly Chores

Weekly Chores

Weekly Chores

Notes

Season Checklist

Monthly Planner

Weekly Chores

Weekly Chores

Weekly Chores

Weekly Chores

Weekly Chores	

Monthly Planner

Weekly Chores

Weekly Chores

Weekly Chores

Weekly Chores

Gardening Expenses

Date	Item	Cost	Notes

Gardening Expenses

Date	Item	Cost	Notes

Gardening Expenses

Date	Item	Cost	Notes

Gardening Expenses

Date	Item	Cost	Notes

Planting Tracker

Plant	Quantity	Start	Transplant	Spacing	Harvest date

Planting Tracker

Plant	Quantity	Start	Transplant	Spacing	Harvest date

Planting Tracker

Plant	Quantity	Start	Transplant	Spacing	Harvest date

Planting Tracker

Plant	Quantity	Start	Transplant	Spacing	Harvest date

Planting Tracker

Plant	Quantity	Start	Transplant	Spacing	Harvest date

Planting Tracker

Plant	Quantity	Start	Transplant	Spacing	Harvest date

Garden Year in Review

What was the best plants and harvests?

What needs improvement?

Next year's Garden wishes

What else?

Notes

Notes

Notes

Notes

Notes

Notes

Notes

Notes